GUIDED FILL IN THE BLANK JOURNAL
FOR DAD

I0617041

MY DAD
ROCKS

101 REASONS WHY I LOVE YOU, DAD

YOU WILL ROCK BOOKS

DEDICATION

To all the dads out there who show up for their kids every single day.

To the dads who stay up late working on science projects.

To the dads who are the biggest cheerleads.

To the dads who have tough conversations.

To the dads who would do anything for their kid.

This is for you!

DEAR,

_____

This journal is for you.

Here are 101 reasons why I love you,
Dad.

LOVE,

_____

HOW TO USE THIS BOOK

Hi, there!

This is the book speaking to you.

All of my prompts are fill-in-the-blank, so you can start on any page!

The only rule is to be creative and have fun.

Now go show your dad how much you love him!

MY GIFT TO YOU

One last thing before we get started.

To keep this short and sweet, I wanted to give you something.

You've already done more than most by buying this book for your dad and showing him your gratitude.

So, the least I could do is give you this free guide on **14 Easy DIY Gifts For Dad That He'll Love**

MY GIFT TO YOU

Scan the QR code
below to access it.

All right, enough chit-chat.

Let's dive in for real this time!

LOVE

The lovey ones.

"ANYONE CAN
BE A FATHER,
BUT IT TAKES
SOMEONE SPECIAL
TO BE A DAD."

-WADE BOGGS

LOVE

1. YOUR IMPACT ON MY LIFE IS BEST DESCRIBED AS

_____

_____

_____

2. HAVING YOUR LOVE IN MY LIFE MAKES ME FEEL

_____

_____

_____

3. ONE THING I'VE LEARNED ABOUT YOU THAT SURPRISED ME IS

_____

_____

_____

4. IF I HAD TO DESCRIBE YOUR ROLE IN MY LIFE, I'D SAY

_____

_____

_____

_____

5. YOU'VE ALWAYS INSPIRED ME TO BELIEVE IN

_____

_____

_____

6. THE WAY YOU APPROACH _____

_____

_____

HAS CHANGED THE WAY I THINK.

7. I LOVED THE DAY THAT WE WENT TO THE

_____

_____

_____

8. YOUR PERSEVERANCE THROUGH _____

_____

_____

HAS BEEN A GUIDING EXAMPLE FOR ME.

9. THE MOST UNEXPECTED LESSON I'VE LEARNED FROM YOU IS

_____

_____

_____

10. THE WAY YOU'VE BALANCED_____

_____

_____

_____

IS SOMETHING I DEEPLY ADMIRE.

11. IF I COULD SUMMARIZE YOUR PARENTING STYLE IN ONE SENTENCE, IT WOULD BE

_____

_____

_____

12. YOU'VE INSPIRED ME TO WORK HARDER AT

_____

_____

_____

13. A TIME WHEN YOU SHOWED INCREDIBLE STRENGTH WAS WHEN

_____

_____

_____

14. THE WAY YOU'VE GUIDED ME THROUGH

_____

_____

_____

HAS BEEN LIFE-CHANGING.

15. IF I COULD BE MORE LIKE YOU AT ONE THING, IT WOULD BE

_____

_____

_____

16. THE WAY YOU'VE BUILT RELATIONSHIPS WITH

_____

_____

_____

_____ **HAS TAUGHT ME SO MUCH.**

17. GROWING UP, I FELT YOUR LOVE THE MOST WHEN WE

_____

_____

_____

18. THREE THINGS I LOVE MOST ABOUT YOU ARE

1 _____

2 _____

3 _____

19. A WAY YOU'VE HELPED ME THAT I'LL NEVER FORGET IS

_____

_____

_____

20. YOUR ABILITY TO STAY POSITIVE DURING

_____ IS SOMETHING I ASPIRE

TO BE.

21. A TIME YOU ENCOURAGED ME WHEN I NEEDED IT MOST WAS

_____

_____

_____

22. YOU'VE ALWAYS SHOWN ME THAT _____

IS WORTH FIGHTING FOR.

23. YOUR LOVE HAS BEEN THE FOUNDATION FOR

_____ IN MY LIFE.

24. WHEN I THINK ABOUT OUR RELATIONSHIP THE FEELINGS THAT COME UP ARE

_____

_____

_____

25. EVEN THOUGH WE MIGHT FIGHT SOMETIMES, I NEED YOU TO KNOW

_____

_____

_____

26. BEING AROUND YOUR PRESENCE MAKES ME FEEL

_____

_____

_____

HUMOR

The funny ones.

"WHY DID THE DAD
BRING A PENCIL
TO BED?"

BECAUSE HE
WANTED
TO DRAW
THE CURTAINS!

HUMOR

27. THE FUNNIEST "DAD JOKE" YOU'VE EVER TOLD IS

_____

_____

_____

28. A TIME WHEN YOUR ADVICE HILARIOUSLY BACKFIRED WAS

_____

_____

_____

29. A MOMENT WHERE WE BOTH COULDN'T STOP LAUGHING WAS WHEN

_____

_____

_____

30. YOUR REACTION TO _____

_____

_____

STILL MAKES ME LAUGH EVERY TIME I THINK ABOUT IT.

31. IF THERE WERE AN OLYMPIC EVENT FOR

_____, YOU'D TAKE HOME THE GOLD MEDAL.

32. NOW THAT I'M OLDER, IT'S TIME I TELL YOU ABOUT

_____

_____

_____

_____

33. THE TIME YOU TRIED TO _____

_____

WILL ALWAYS BE A FAVORITE MEMORY OF MINE.

34. YOU ONCE SAID _____

_____

_____

AND I'M STILL LAUGHING ABOUT IT TO THIS DAY.

35. YOUR MOST CREATIVE EXCUSE FOR _____

WAS _____

_____

AND IT WAS PURE COMEDY GOLD.

36. IF I COULD BOTTLE YOUR LAUGH, IT WOULD

SOUND LIKE _____ **AND IT WOULD SELL FOR**

_____

37. THE TIME YOU _____ **INSTEAD OF**

_____ **WAS CLASSIC DAD LOGIC.**

38. YOUR BEST REACTION TO A SURPRISE WAS WHEN

_____

_____

_____

39. IF DAD REFLEXES WERE A SPORT, YOUR GREATEST SAVE WAS WHEN

_____

_____

_____

40. THE FUNNIEST MISUNDERSTANDING WE'VE EVER HAD WAS ABOUT

_____

_____

_____

41. A PHRASE YOU ALWAYS SAY THAT I'LL NEVER

FORGET IS " _____ ."

42. THE BEST NICKNAME YOU'VE EVER GIVEN ME IS

_____ , AND I SECRETLY LOVE IT.

43. YOU TRIED TO TEACH ME _____

_____

ONCE, AND WE BOTH ENDED UP LAUGHING TOO

HARD TO FINISH.

44. YOUR ABILITY TO TURN

_____

_____

INTO A MESS NEVER FAILS TO MAKE ME GIGGLE.

45. THE WAY YOU _____ DURING

FAMILY TIME IS ALWAYS HILARIOUS.

46. IF YOU WERE A SITCOM CHARACTER, YOUR

CATCHPHRASE WOULD BE " _____ ."

GRATITUDE

The grateful ones.

"ENJOY THE LITTLE THINGS, FOR ONE DAY YOU MAY LOOK BACK AND REALIZE THEY WERE THE BIG THINGS."

-ROBERT BRAULT

GRATITUDE

47. THE BEST LESSON YOU'VE EVER TAUGHT ME IS

_____

_____

_____

48. YOUR SUPPORT DURING

_____

_____

HAS MEANT MORE TO ME THAN WORDS CAN SAY.

49. A TIME WHEN YOU MADE ME FEEL INCREDIBLY LOVED WAS WHEN

_____

_____

_____

50. I ADMIRE YOUR ABILITY TO

_____

_____

AND I'M SO GRATEFUL FOR IT.

51. THE WAY YOU'VE ALWAYS SHOWN UP FOR ME

DURING _____ MAKES ME SO THANKFUL.

52. IF I COULD THANK YOU FOR ONE MOMENT IN PARTICULAR, IT WOULD BE WHEN

_____

_____

_____

_____

53. YOU'VE MADE ME FEEL SAFE BY ALWAYS

_____

_____

_____

54. YOUR WISDOM ABOUT _____

HAS SHAPED MY OUTLOOK ON LIFE.

55. YOU'VE TAUGHT ME TO APPRECIATE

_____

_____

_____

AND I'LL ALWAYS BE GRATEFUL FOR THAT.

56. I'M GRATEFUL YOU'VE SACRIFICED

_____

_____

_____

IN ORDER FOR ME TO HAVE A BETTER LIFE.

57. YOU'VE TAUGHT ME HOW TO HANDLE LIFE CHALLENGES LIKE

_____

_____

_____

WITH STRENGTH AND GRACE.

58. YOUR EXAMPLE HAS SHOWN ME THE IMPORTANCE OF

_____

_____

_____

59. I'M SO GRATEFUL FOR HOW YOU'VE TAUGHT ME TO VALUE

_____

_____

_____

60. THE WAY YOU'VE HANDLED _____

HAS BEEN AN INCREDIBLE INSPIRATION.

61. IF I COULD DESCRIBE HOW GRATEFUL I AM FOR

YOU IN ONE WORD, IT WOULD BE " _____ ."

62. YOUR ABILITY TO STAY CALM DURING

_____

_____

_____

HAS TAUGHT ME SO MUCH.

63. A TIME WHEN YOU WENT OUT OF YOUR WAY TO HELP ME WAS

_____

_____

_____

64. YOU'VE ALWAYS CHALLENGED ME TO

_____

_____

65. YOU'VE TAUGHT ME THE IMPORTANCE OF

_____

_____

_____

AND I CARRY IT WITH ME EVERY DAY.

66. YOUR GENEROSITY DURING

_____

_____

IS SOMETHING I'LL ALWAYS REMEMBER.

67. I'LL NEVER STOP BEING GRATEFUL FOR THE WAY YOU'VE SUPPORTED ME IN

_____

_____

_____

68. YOU'VE SHOWN ME WHAT IT MEANS TO TRULY CARE FOR OTHERS BY

_____

_____

_____

69. THE WAY YOU'VE CELEBRATED _____

_____

_____

WITH ME HAS ALWAYS MADE ME FEEL SO GRATEFUL.

70. YOUR DEDICATION TO _____

_____

_____

HAS INSPIRED ME BEYOND WORDS.

71. I'M THANKFUL FOR HOW YOU'VE HELPED ME GROW IN

_____

_____

_____

MEMORIES

The memorable ones.

"AND YET
MEMORIES ARE
THE MOST
PRECIOUS THINGS
WE'LL EVER HAVE."

-UNKNOWN

MEMORIES

72. THE BEST ADVICE YOU'VE EVER GIVEN ME WAS

_____

_____

_____

73. A LESSON I LEARNED FROM WATCHING YOU IS

_____

_____

_____

74. ONE THING YOU'VE ALWAYS DONE THAT'S MADE ME FEEL LOVED IS

_____

_____

_____

75. YOU'VE TAUGHT ME THE IMPORTANCE OF

_____ **IN LIFE.**

76. THE MOST SELFLESS THING YOU'VE EVER DONE FOR ME WAS

_____

_____

_____

77. YOU'VE SHOWN ME HOW TO STAY STRONG BY

_____

_____

_____

78. THE HAPPIEST I'VE EVER SEEN YOU WAS WHEN

_____

_____

_____

79. IF I COULD THANK YOU FOR ONE THING, IT WOULD BE

_____

_____

_____

80. THE WAY YOU SUPPORT ME THROUGH

_____ **HAS MADE ALL THE DIFFERENCE.**

81. A QUIET MOMENT WE SHARED THAT I'LL NEVER FORGET WAS WHEN

_____

_____

_____

82. YOU'VE DEMONSTRATED THE IMPORTANCE OF

_____ IN A WAY I'LL NEVER FORGET.

83. ONE OF MY FAVORITE THINGS ABOUT YOU IS

_____

_____

_____

84. A TIME WHEN YOUR KINDNESS AMAZED ME WAS

_____

_____

_____

85. YOU'VE ALWAYS BELIEVED IN ME, EVEN WHEN I DOUBTED

_____

_____

_____

86. IF I COULD DESCRIBE YOUR LOVE IN ONE SENTENCE, IT WOULD BE

_____

_____

_____

87. THE WAY YOU'VE TAUGHT ME ABOUT

_____ **HAS SHAPED WHO I AM.**

88. I FEEL PROUD TO BE YOUR CHILD BECAUSE

_____

_____

_____

89. YOUR DETERMINATION DURING

_____

_____

_____

HAS INSPIRED ME MORE THAN YOU KNOW.

90. THE MOST SURPRISING ADVICE YOU'VE EVER GIVEN ME WAS

_____

_____

_____

91. YOU'VE ALWAYS BEEN MY ROLE MODEL BECAUSE OF

_____

_____

_____

92. A MOMENT I'VE ALWAYS CHERISHED IS WHEN YOU

_____

_____

_____

93. YOU'VE SHOWN ME THE MEANING OF FAMILY BY

_____

_____

_____

94. YOUR ENCOURAGEMENT DURING _____

GAVE ME THE STRENGTH TO KEEP GOING.

95. IF I COULD RELIVE ONE DAY WITH YOU, IT WOULD BE

_____

_____

_____

96. THE TIME YOU _____

_____

LIVES RENT-FREE IN MY MEMORY BECAUSE,

_____

97. YOU LEFT A HANDPRINT ON MY HEART WHEN YOU

_____

_____

_____

98. ONE THING I HOPE TO PASS DOWN TO MY KIDS THAT I LEARNED FROM YOU IS

_____

_____

_____

99. THE MOMENT THAT MADE ME FEEL THE MOST GRATEFUL FOR YOU WAS WHEN

_____

_____

_____

100. EVERY TIME WE GO HERE TOGETHER, IT MAKES ME REMEMBER

_____

_____

_____

_____

SPECIAL

The special one.

"DAD'S ROCK!"

-LEXI KAZ

SPECIAL

101. I LOVE YOU DAD BECAUSE

_____

_____

_____

_____

_____

A FINAL THANK You

_____

_____

_____

_____

LOVE,

_____

#1 DAD OF THE YEAR AWARD

We hope you enjoyed completing this book!

You've given your dad something he'll cherish forever.

So I have **one** last question for you.

Do you feel he's the **#1 Dad of the Year?**

Hopefully, you said yes!

#1 DAD OF THE YEAR AWARD

If you did say yes, please do the following!

1. Post a video of your dad's reaction to giving him this book.

2. Tag us on **TikTok @Youwillrockbooks**

3. Mention why you believe he deserves to win the **#1 Dad of the Year Award.**

The winner will receive a cash prize from **You Will Rock Books** to further our mission of supporting Fathers everywhere.

#1 DAD OF THE YEAR AWARD

The best video submission will win the **#1 Dad of the Year Award.**

Now go give him this book!

For more information on the **#1 Dad of the Year Award**, go to www.Youwillrock.com

Or email us any questions at info@youwillrock.com

PASS IT ON!

If you enjoyed our book, please leave us an honest review from wherever you purchased it.

This way, another Dad can get the love he deserves.

You rock!

THE END.

www.ingramcontent.com/pod-product-compliance
Lightning Source LLC
Chambersburg PA
CBHW051644120626
46551CB00015B/2204